YOUR KNOWLEDGE HAS VALUE

AF168048

- We will publish your bachelor's and master's thesis, essays and papers

- Your own eBook and book - sold worldwide in all relevant shops

- Earn money with each sale

Upload your text at www.GRIN.com and publish for free

Bibliographic information published by the German National Library:

The German National Library lists this publication in the National Bibliography; detailed bibliographic data are available on the Internet at http://dnb.dnb.de .

This book is copyright material and must not be copied, reproduced, transferred, distributed, leased, licensed or publicly performed or used in any way except as specifically permitted in writing by the publishers, as allowed under the terms and conditions under which it was purchased or as strictly permitted by applicable copyright law. Any unauthorized distribution or use of this text may be a direct infringement of the author s and publisher s rights and those responsible may be liable in law accordingly.

Imprint:

Copyright © 2020 GRIN Verlag
Print and binding: Books on Demand GmbH, Norderstedt Germany
ISBN: 9783346242853

This book at GRIN:

https://www.grin.com/document/921009

Kubiat Udo

Information Retrieval. An Ontology-based Approach

GRIN Verlag

GRIN - Your knowledge has value

Since its foundation in 1998, GRIN has specialized in publishing academic texts by students, college teachers and other academics as e-book and printed book. The website www.grin.com is an ideal platform for presenting term papers, final papers, scientific essays, dissertations and specialist books.

Visit us on the internet:

http://www.grin.com/

http://www.facebook.com/grincom

http://www.twitter.com/grin_com

Information Retrieval; ontology-based approach.

By

Kubiat Udo

Abstract

Information shared over the web keeps escalating gradually and rapidly. Due to this fast and steady growth, well-known problems are associated with retrieving desired information when needed. However, a few initiatives were introduced in the previous decade with the development of search engine technology. The search engine technology aids in the collection, storage and pre-processing a wide range of information to deliver relevant resources instantly in response to users' needs. Nevertheless, users sometimes need more effort to obtain desired information. This paper discusses the concept of information retrieval with some emphasis on the different information retrieval models. Furthermore, this paper will describe how documents are analyzed and ranked using different models.

Keywords: Ontology, Information Retrieval, Query processing, Indexing, Search, Ranking.

1

1. Introduction

The rising amount of useful information being shared over the web requires adequate techniques for effective search and retrieval. As such, information such as audio, video, images and textual data must be accommodated. A significant problem is that users can easily be inundated with the quantity of information available.

The transfer of irrelevant information such as text, audio, video retrieved by an information retrieval system to the user wastes network bandwidth and at times frustrates users. This is because of inaccuracies, in the illustration of the documents stored in the database, in addition to the ambiguity in user queries. These factors contribute to the presentation of irrelevant information to the user. As such, the key problem to be addressed in information retrieval is the development of a search strategy which will ensure the delivery of a minimum amount of irrelevant information to the user when compared to the amount of relevant information rendered.

2. Research Methodology

The research methodology adopted in this paper is based on case studies. Emphases are made on proper background analysis of a limited number of events and their relationships.

3. Information Retrieval Process

The main goal of an Information Retrieval (IR) System can be defined as the representation, storage, organization of, and access to information items (Ribeiro & Baeza, 1999).

Information retrieval systems operate based on a given set of documents, that are pre-processed according to user queries, ranked based on their relevance and presented to the user according to their relevance degree.

This section of the paper shall provide briefly the description of components, tasks and resources involved in IR systems. An abstract view of the elements is displayed in Figure 3.1.

Figure 3.1 **The Information Retrieval Process** (Sanchez,2009).

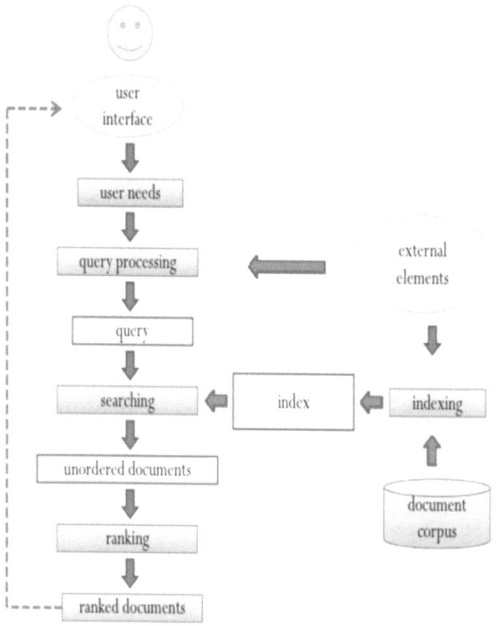

3.1. Input

An Information Retrieval system accepts two types of input. These inputs are categorized into the user needs and the information items. However, the process of information retrieval begins when the user conveys his information need (*User needs*) to the system. This information is often expressed as a search string which can also be expressed in other formats. An example of which would be multimedia retrieval where information needed by the user could include video clips, images and sound.

Furthermore, the information items are the elements, which are being retrieved as an answer to a query. However, an information item is classified by its formats (textual document, image, audio, video, etc) and its granularity (web page, paragraph, sentence, etc).

3.2. Output

The main output returned by an Information Retrieval system is a ranked list of information items.

The output consists of a sorted list of information items irrespective of their formats, for example, texts, audios, videos etc. However, considering the structure of the output returned, an outsized categorization can be made distinguishing systems that return unstructured information i.e., Items with arbitrary structure and syntax, for example, free text documents and those that return specifically structured information. For example, the relational database objects. Moreover, systems that return structured information as output are often categorized as *information retrieval systems.*

3.3. Process

According to an article by (Croft & Harper, 1993), three main processes occurs during the retrieval of information. These three processes are indexing, query processing and searching & ranking.

Indexing

This is the extraction of item content features and descriptors into a logical representation (Croft & Harper, 1993). It is indispensable to pre-process the information items to determine the element to be used as an index objects, because some words carry more meaning than others. There are reliable data structures developed to speed up the search process especially when large collections of items are involved. An example of such is the inverted file indexing structure commonly used in text retrieval. The whole concept behind the inverted file indexing structure is that, search is done based on vocabulary and term occurrences. The vocabulary is the set of words in a text while the list of word appearance in the database is the occurrence.

Query processing

The query is the user needs. It is compiled in an internal format. During a textual retrieval, the same algorithm used in selecting the index objects during the indexing process is adopted to pre-process the query term.

Search & Ranking

User queries are matched based on the information items. During this operation, a set of possible information item is returned as a response to the user query. However, this operation varies based on the format of the information item. It could be an audio, video, or textual form. For example, during a classic text retrieval process, information items are matched based on the set of index terms. Moreover, a similar process may occur during a multimedia retrieval process. Once information items are returned, not all items are considered relevant to the user. The items are ranked by a ranking algorithm. The stage of ranking aims at predicting which items are relevant to the user. As such, the ranking algorithm can be considered the core of IR systems as it influences the system performance in a way.

4. Information Retrieval Models

The algorithm used in ranking is the main component of the information retrieval system. The algorithm operates based on a basic premise regarding the notion of document relevance. The three most common models, which form the basis for other information retrieval models, are the Boolean, Vector and Probabilistic models. These models can be further developed or combined for enhanced Information retrieval.

According to the definitions offered in (Baeza & Ribeiro, 1999& Sanchez, 2009) the Information Retrieval model are quadruple, [D, Q, F, sim], where:

- D is a set of (logical representations of) documents.
- Q is a set of (logical representations of) queries.
- F is a framework for modeling documents, queries, and their relationships.

• Sim: Q × D → U is a ranking function that defines an association between queries and documents, where U is a totally ordered set (commonly [0,1], or P, or a subset thereof). This ranking and the total order in U defines an order in the set of documents, for a fixed query.

To develop an ontology, we consider how best the user information needs and documents will be represented.

However, in accordance to these representations, the structure in which they can be formed is then apprehended. This structure should also stipulate the inkling for creating a ranking function. Here, is an example, for the classic Boolean model, the structure (framework) is made of sets of documents and the standard operaon sets. For the classic vector-space model, it is made of a t-dimensional v-space and linear algebra functions on vectors. For the classic probabilistic model, the framework is made of sets, standard probability operations, and the Bayes' theorem (Sanchez, 2009). This paper will elaborate more on the boolean, vector and probabilistic ontologies of information retrieval.

Boolean Model

In the Boolean model, document and queries are represented as a set of index terms. The Boolean model is the most commonly used model due to its ease of implementation. In the Boolean model, documents and user queries are represented as a set of index terms. Documents that include the index terms contained within user queries are returned as search results. The Boolean model fails to rank documents which is a problem especially if the retrieved documents are in 1000s. Most common search engines employ the boolean model due to its simplicity, but the model is usually enhanced to allow for ranking documents retrieved. Furthermore, the Boolean model can be categorized into the standard, smart and extended Boolean models.

The *standard Boolean* aims to capture contextual information. The method adopted in this model is based on proximity, truncation and the boolean functions (AND, OR, NOT). Some key advantages of this model include efficiency in computation and ease in implementation. However, users find difficulties in constructing boolean queries as the logical operators AND, OR, NOT represent different meanings when used in queries.

The *smart Boolean* aims to provide solutions to a few limitations of the standard or traditional Boolean model. This model aims to structure the re-formulation process of searching. It adopts the use of contextual knowledge-base to enhance the clarity of Boolean expressions. However, there is no need for Boolean operators as the logical operators in statements are automatically translated into Boolean topic representation.

The *extended Boolean* aims to provide ranking of relevant documents retrieved in response to user queries. The fuzzy logic is applied in this model. Unlike the traditional Boolean where there exist only two-valued logic, TRUE and FALSE, the extended Boolean has been developed to handle more than two valued logic. In the fuzzy logic, a document can be retrieved on the concept of partial truth where the truth value of a documemt can range between completely TRUE and completely FALSE. However, the fuzzy logic allows approximation of data retrieved, compared to the classic Boolean model. Furthermore, the fuzzy logic and probabilistic logic are similar because they both have truth values ranging between 0 and 1. Nevertheless, the fuzzy logic retrieves information based on the degree's of truth while the probability logic depends on the percentage of likelihood found in a document. Based on these descriptions, the fuzzy and probability logic are both mathematically similar, but conceptually distinct.

Vector-space Model

In the Vector-space model, documents and queries are represented as vectors in a t-dimensional space. The Vector-space model allows for ranking of documents. This model takes two weights into consideration when ranking retrieved documents: term frequency and document frequency. Term frequency denotes the number of times a term within the search query appears within a document. The higher the term frequency, the more relevant the document is. Document frequency denotes the number of documents (in a collection) which contain a term within the query search. The higher the document frequency, the less relevant the search term. When a search query contains more than one term, document frequency ascribes more weight to the rarer terms within the search query. In the Vector-space model, queries and documents are represented as vectors based on both weighting schemes. Cosine similarity is used to determine the cosine of the angle between the document and query, and the ranking of retrieved documents is done based on this similarity.

Probabilistic Model

In the basic probabilistic model, documents and queries representations are ranked based on the probability theory. According to the probability ranking principle, uncertainties exist in the representation of information needs and documents. One source of evidence that is used by the probabilistic retrieval method is the Bayesian inference network. The Bayesian network in IR models compute the probability of relevance given a document and query. The two important models of the Bayesian Network are the Belief network model and the Bayesian network retrieval model. According to the Bayesian system, an inference network consists of a directed acyclic dependency graph. The edges of the graph denote dependencies between the propositions represented by the nodes. The inference network consists of an indexing vocabulary presented as a concept network, document network and the information need presented as a query network. The idea of the Bayesian system is that the concept network is used as an interface between documents and queries. However, the key features are; each index term and document represented as nodes in the network and there are links connecting each document node with all the term nodes. Moreover, the model differs in the direction of the arc and the additional arc which is the relationship between documents and terms. Illustrated below is a simple Bayesian Network-based retrieval model.

Figure 4.1 **The Bayesian Network-Based Retrieval Model**

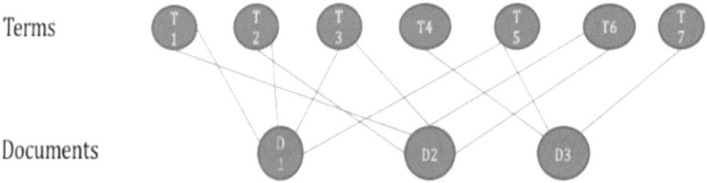

Furthermore, a key problem encounted by the Bayesian inference network is the time and space it requires to assess the distributions and to store them. The conditional probability per node is exponential with the parent nodes. (Howard Turtle, 1991)

5. Information Retrieval Evaluation

Due to the incessant development of information over the web, IR performance has become progressively more vital. Subsequently, it has become of utmost necessity that commercial developers and vendors of new information products carefully study the various competetive advantages proffered by their products. However, considering information retrieval evaluation, this paper aims at rendering an analysis of how well the system works. There are mainly three types of evaluation of information retrieval systems (Baeza, Ribeiro, 1999 & Sanchez, 2009): The first type is considered as the functional evaluation. In the functional evaluation, the specified system functionalities are tested independently. However, it is aimed at evaluating the user's satisfaction of the system. The second type is the performance evaluation. This is the most common procedures of system performance evaluation. It is aimed at evaluating how effective the system ranks documents in accordance to time and space (the shorter the response time, the smaller the space used, the better the system is considered to be). The third type is the *retrieval performance evaluation*. This evaluation measures the effectiveness of the IR system in accordance to user queries. Furthermore, there are two types of retrieval performance evaluation. It is categorized into the user and system based retrieval performance evaluations. However, in this paper, more emphasis will be made on the system-based performance evaluation.

The system-based performance evaluation discussed in this paper shall be in accordance with the Cranfield Evaluation Paradigm. In adoption of the Cranfield Evaluation Paradigm, experiments are carried out based on test collections. The test collections include documents, a few sample queries and a set of relevant documents manually identified for each sample query. In the Cranfield Evaluation Paradigm, the test collections aid in comparison of the different Information Retrieval approaches using various evaluation measures. (Cleverdon, 1991)

Evalution Metrics

Considering an Information Retrieval technique, the evaluation metrics quantifies the similarities between a set of relevant and irrelevant documents retrieved in response to a query. There are several evaluation metrics, yet none has proven satisfactory. This is because information retrieval performance evaluation is highly dependent on the user. These evaluations are performed using the test collections. However, because all documents are not classified into relevant classes in the database, the retrieved information is usually in binary form (relevant or irrelevant).

The two most commonly used evaluation metrics are the precision and recall.

Precision & Recall

Precision can be defined as the fraction of documents that are relevant while Recall is the fraction of all relevant documents retrieved. The precision and recall measures were developed to improve information retrieval based on sets with respect to a given query. Illustrated in table 2.1 is an example of precision and recall.

Table 2.1 **Recall-Precision example.**

Rank	Document #	Relevant?
1	34	
2	3	Yes
3	45	
4	270	
5	63	Yes
6	1	Yes
7	89	Yes

However, during information retrieval, documents can be sub divided into sets based on the relevance of the document retrieved. Below is a tabular display of the sub sets in which a document can be partitioned.

Table 2.2 **Document Partitions.**

Sub sets	A Relevant document	An Irrelevant document
Document Retrieved	A	B
Document Not Retrieved	C	D

Following the sub sets in which a document can be categorized into, precision and recall can be represented mathematically as follows;

$$Precision = \frac{A}{A \cup B}$$

Figure 5.1

$$Recall = \frac{A}{A \cup C}$$

Figure 5.2

There exist a tradeoff between recall and precision. An increase in recall leads to a decrease in precision. The values of the recall and precision are 0 and 1. This technique of information retrieval evaluation is a set based measure. It is commonly used in the evaluation of an unranked set of documents retrieved. Nevertheless, the case is slightly different when evaluating a ranked list of documents, as the recall-precision curves are used. In a ranked list, at each point of recall, the precision can be measured. However, when a relevant document is retrieved, there is a significant increase in recall. Below is a figure illustrating the trade-off between recall and precision.

Figure 5.3 **The Trade-off between Recall and Precision** (Sanchez,2009).

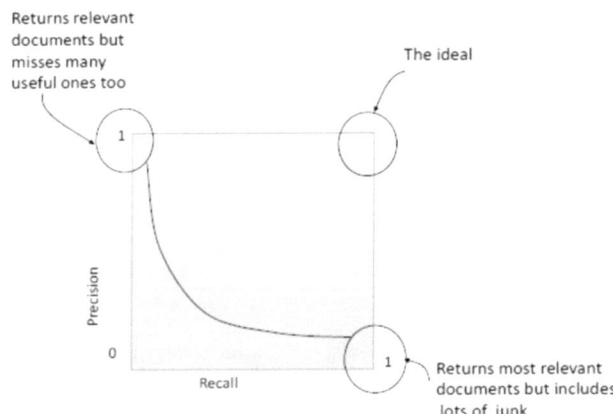

Furthermore, the recall–precision graph shows the combination of recall and precision as measures of a ranked retrieval, whereby precision is measured at various points of recall. To derive the recall and precision graph, some form of interpolation is introduced. For example, setting precision at a given point and recall level to the highest subsequent precision. Interpolation allows precision to remain unchanged or decrease as recall increases. However, an interpolated recall-precision curve offers the possibility of the system to deliver more useful information, in response to a query on a topic. Moreover, the assumption that the ranking offered by a recall-precision curve includes all, or majority of, relevant documents are no more realistic (Webber, 2010). Figure 5.4 illustrates an interpolated recall-precision graph of a ranking performed by a search algorithm compared to an actual recall-precision curve.

Figure 5.4 **Recall-Precision calculation** (Webber,2010).

	Rank									
	1	2	3	4	5	6	7	8	9	10
r_i	1	0	0	1	1	0	0	0	1	0
R@i	0.25	0.25	0.25	0.5	0.75	0.75	0.75	0.75	1	1
P@i	1	0.5	0.33	0.5	**0.6**	0.5	0.43	0.38	**0.44**	0.4

(a) Actual recall-precision

Recall	0.0	0.1	0.2	0.3	0.4	0.5	0.6	0.7	0.8	0.9	1.0
Precision	1	1	1	0.6	0.6	0.6	0.6	0.6	0.44	0.44	0.44

(b) Eleven-point interpolated recall-precision

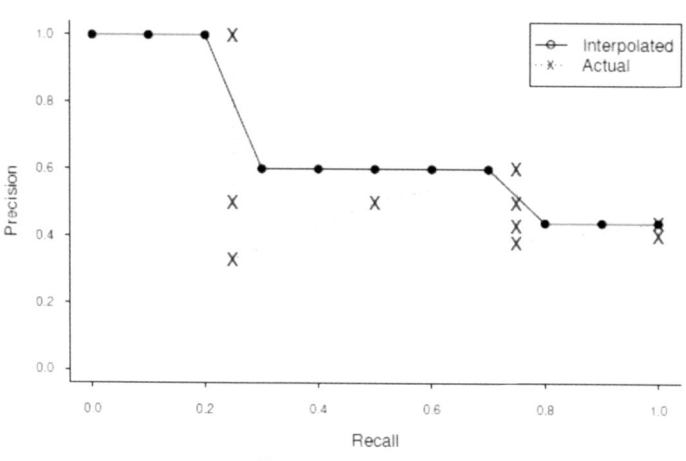

(c) Recall–precision curve

6 Conclusion

Considering the importance of information, adequate measures should be taken to improve the search mechanisms currently adopted in retrieving information from the web. However, without the development of enhanced information retrieval systems, to solve the various limitations in existing models used for retrieving information on the web, users will find it cumbersome when retrieving desired information. Moreover, the current ontologies can be further developed or combined for enhanced information retrieval. Furthermore, current research offers the possibility of solving the problems associated with information retrieval based on literal strings rather than conceptual meaning, with the adoption of semantics for enhanced information retrieval.

Reference

[1] Cleverdon, C. (1991). *The significance of the Cranfield tests on index languages.* Chicago, Illinois, USA.

[2] Howard Turtle, W. B. (1991). Evaluation of an Inference Network-Based Retrieval Model.

[3] *Knowledge-based and statistical approaches to text retrieval*1993IEEE

[4] Modern Information Retrieval1999

[5] *Semantically enhanced Information Retrieval: an ontology-based approach*2009Madrid

[6] Webber, W. E. (2010). Measurement in Information Retrieval Evaluation. In A. S. Buckley, & E. Voorhees, *Retrieval System Evaluation* (p. Chapter 3).

YOUR KNOWLEDGE HAS VALUE

- We will publish your bachelor's and master's thesis, essays and papers

- Your own eBook and book - sold worldwide in all relevant shops

- Earn money with each sale

Upload your text at www.GRIN.com
and publish for free